Mom-

mush to you from me -

Tina

Y0-CAT-191

Japanese Love Poems

JAPANESE
LOVE
POEMS

Edited by Jean Bennett

Illustrated by Scott Cumming

DOUBLEDAY & COMPANY, INC.
Garden City, New York
1976

DESIGNED BY LAURENCE ALEXANDER

Library of Congress Cataloging in Publication Data

Main entry under title:

Japanese love poems.

Includes index.
1. Love poetry, Japanese—Translations into English.
2. Love poetry, English—Translations from Japanese.
I. Bennett, Jean, 1947–
PL782.E3J34   895.6′1′1080354
ISBN: 0-385-03085-1
Library of Congress Catalog Card Number 76–2753

Copyright © *1976 by Doubleday & Company, Inc.*

ALL RIGHTS RESERVED

PRINTED IN THE UNITED STATES OF AMERICA

FIRST EDITION

ACKNOWLEDGMENTS

The editor and publisher are grateful to the following publishers and individuals for permission to include in this volume the selections listed below:

Doubleday & Company, Inc., for the poems appearing on pages 25, 57, and 58, from *The Confessions of Lady Nijō*, translated from the Japanese by Karen Brazell. Translation copyright © 1973 by Karen Brazell.
Friendship Press for the poems appearing on pages 2, 26, 59, and 96, from *Songs from the Land of Dawn*, by Toyohiko Kagawa and other Japanese poets, copyright © 1949 by Friendship Press.

iv

Kodansha International for poems appearing on pages 14, 15, 16, 17, 18, 33, 49, 50, 64, 65, 66, 78, 86, and 87, quoted from *The Silent Firefly*, translated by Eric Sackheim, copyright © 1963 by Kodansha International.

Kodansha International for poems appearing on pages 51 and 62, quoted from *Takuboku: Poems to Eat*, translated by Carl Sesar, copyright © 1966 by Kodansha International.

John Murray (Publishers) Ltd. for poems appearing on pages 7, 8, 11, 21, 24, 33, 42, 47, and 60, from *Japanese Poetry*, by Basil Hall Chamberlain.

Mushinsha Limited for poems appearing on pages 13, 48, 63, 77, and 96, from *The Genial Seed: a Japanese Song Cycle*, translated by Frank Hoff, copyright © 1971 in Japan by Mushinsha Limited.

Mushinsha Limited for poems appearing on pages 6, 38, 44, 45, 55, 63, and 93, from *This Wine of Peace, This Wine of Laughter*, translated by Donald Philippi, copyright © 1968 in Japan by Mushinsha Limited.

New Directions Publishing Corporation for poems appearing on pages 2, 3, 4, 5, 24, 26, 38, 47, and 55, from *One Hundred Poems from the Japanese*, by Kenneth Rexroth. All Rights Reserved.

The Oxford University Press for poems appearing on pages 5, 56, 74, 75, and 91, from *A Hundred Verses from Old Japan*, translated by William N. Porter.

William Packard for the passage appearing on page 9, from *Ikkaku Sennin*, a Japanese Noh play adapted by William Packard from the translation by Frank Hoff, in *Four Classical Asian Plays*, edited by Vera R. Irwin, published by Penguin Books.

The Estate of Curtis Hidden Page for the poems appearing on pages 18, 25, 46, 54, and 87, from *Japanese Poetry, an Historical Essay with Two Hundred and Thirty Translations*, by Curtis Hidden Page, published by Houghton Mifflin Company, copyright © 1923.

Stanford University Press for poems appearing on pages 4, 6, 34, 43, 45, 46, 54, 56, 59, 72, and 73, reprinted from *An Introduction to Japanese Court Poetry* by Earl Miner, with translations by the author and Robert H. Brower, copyright © 1968 by the Board of Trustees of the Leland Stanford Junior University.

Charles E. Tuttle Company, Inc., for poems appearing on pages 13, 14, 67, 79, 80, 81, 82, 83, and 88, from *Comrade Loves of the Samurai and Songs of the Geishas*, translated by E. Powys Mathers, copyright © 1972 in Japan by Charles E. Tuttle Company, Inc.

Charles E. Tuttle Company, Inc., for "The Bamboo Flute by the Shore," on page 94, from *A History of Japanese Literature*, by W. G. Aston, copyright © 1972 in Japan by Charles E. Tuttle Company, Inc.

Walker & Company, Inc., New York, N.Y., for poems appearing on pages 19, 29, 43, and 51, from the book *Japanese Literature*, by Roger Bersihand, translated from the French by Unity Evans, copyright © 1965 by Walker & Company.

CONTENTS

PREFACE

That the Japanese love poetry of over a thousand years ago can speak as truly to the modern heart and mind of the essential nature of love as any written today is a tribute to the Japanese sensibility, an ability to feel deeply and to put that feeling into words directly and simply. The love poems included in this volume are by Japan's classic poets, ancient and modern, and they reveal a deep understanding of love in all its moods and aspects.

Ancient Japanese poetry was the poetry of the court, which enjoyed two distinct kinds of love: marital and illicit. Because most marriages were arranged in childhood, marital love was often a deep affection and regard which grew after marriage, forming an unbreakable bond. Many of the poems in this volume express devotion in marriage (which is cherished and idealized), the sorrow of parting from a spouse, or the joy of reunion. On the other hand, love affairs were common (most ladies of letters were courtesans), and a great deal of Japanese poetry refers to this kind of love. Clandestine meetings, the sacrifice and suffering that must be endured for one night of illicit love, the pain of separation in the early hours of the morning, the agony of unrequited love for all common themes, allowing for the expression of great passion which by its very nature is short-lived.

The Japanese poetic tradition embodies a belief in the *truth* of human feeling; it is a current that is always there, not merely a sporadic outburst of emotion. This strong current of feeling is considered the essence of Japanese poetry, and is called, in Japanese, *aware*.

The poignancy of Japanese love poetry derives largely from two major influences on Japanese thought and understanding: Shintoism and Buddhism. While a profound delight in the pleasures and beauty of this world was the legacy of Shintoism, at the same time Buddhism instilled an awareness of its impermanence: beauty fades, lovers are faithless, love is a dream from which one will eventually awaken. Moreover, in the Buddhist framework love is the "darkness of the heart," an attachment to this world which is thereby a barrier to salvation. It is no wonder that the Japanese experience of love is bittersweet, beauty accompanied by a pervasive melancholy, and it is this quality in particular that goes straight to the heart.

The eighth century was the golden age of Japanese poetry, and by far its greatest poet was Kakinomoto no Hitomaro, who was unique in achieving a balance between inner and outer, man and nature, self and society. Other poets of the first rank were Yamanoe no Okura, Yamabe no Akahito, and Ōtomo no Yakamochi. It was Yakamochi, who looked inward where other poets had looked outward, who led the way in the direction later poets would take. The poets in the *Kokinshū*, the first great imperial anthology (completed about A.D. 905), illuminated for the Japanese the essential experience of love, one of the major themes of this and later anthologies. There were four outstanding poets in the collection: Ono no Komachi, Ariwara no Narihira, Ki no Tomonori, and Ki no Tsurayuki. The love affairs of Komachi, considered Japan's greatest beauty, are legendary, and her poetry is above all passionate. It was Komachi's influence which gave primary importance to the woman's needs and feelings in the literature of courtly love. It was the understanding of the need for both spontaneity and the mastery of an art that could be learned and practiced like any other art which these poets left as a legacy for those who followed them. In the famous words of Tsurayuki in his preface to the *Kokinshū*, poetry "takes root in the human heart and flourishes in the countless leaves of words."

In addition to the poetry of the court, many of the great poems in Japanese are songs that were sung by the Geishas and by field workers planting rice and celebrating fertility in their songs of love and sex.

The following brief outline of the major literary periods will aid in placing the poems in this volume in a chronological perspective:

ARCHAIC PERIOD (*before* A.D. 700)
NARA PERIOD (*eighth century*)
HEIAN, OR CLASSICAL PERIOD (800–1186)
KAMAKURA PERIOD (1187–1332)
NAMBOKU-CHŌ PERIOD (1333–1392)
MUROMACHI PERIOD (1393–1603)
YEDO PERIOD (1604–1867)
TOKYO PERIOD (1868 *to present*)

The poems in this volume are representative of the best poets from the archaic period to the present, and can truly be included among the world's great love poetry.

J. Bennett

Japanese Love Poems

Night;
And a doorway left ajar . . .

Night;
And a doorway left ajar
In the white moonbeams;
For you promised your spirit would come to me, Love,
    In my dreams!

                    Ōtomo no Yakamochi (8TH CENTURY)
                    NARA PERIOD

Gossip grows like weeds
In a summer meadow.
My girl and I
Sleep arm in arm.

              Kakinomoto no Hitomaro (8TH CENTURY)
              NARA PERIOD

Do not smile to yourself
Like a green mountain
With a cloud drifting across it.
People will know we are in love.

Lady Ōtomo no Sakano-e (8TH CENTURY)
NARA PERIOD

Pebbles

Where the Chikuma flows through Shinama,
If but on the pebbles you tread,
I will gather them up, like precious gems,
From the dry river bed.

Anonymous
NARA PERIOD

The memories of long love
Gather like drifting snow,
Poignant as the mandarin ducks,
Who float side by side in sleep.

Lady Murasaki Shikibu (10TH CENTURY)
HEIAN PERIOD

Although my feet
Never cease running to you
On the path of dreams,
Such nights of love are never worth
One glimpse of you in your reality.

Ono no Komachi (9TH CENTURY)
HEIAN PERIOD

My Love

Falling from the ridge
Of high Tsukuba,
The Minano River
At last gathers itself,
Like my love, into
A deep, still pool.

The Emperor Yōzei (868–949)
HEIAN PERIOD

Alas! the blush upon my cheek,
Conceal it as I may,
Proclaims to all that I'm in love,
Till people smile and say—
'Where are thy thoughts today?'

Taira no Kanemori (10TH CENTURY)
HEIAN PERIOD

As it blows on me,
The autumn wind has penetrated
Through my very flesh—
Why did I regard it as a thing
That lacks the color of human love?

Ki no Tomonori (10TH CENTURY)
HEIAN PERIOD

I am at a loss
To say to whom if not to you
I might show these flowers;
For such beauty and such fragrance
Only the best judge is a judge at all.

Ki no Tomonori (10TH CENTURY)
HEIAN PERIOD

My beloved
Must be coming this evening.
For the behavior
Of the spiders on the bamboo-grass
Is striking this evening.

Sung by the Princess So-tōshi,
a favorite of Emperor Ingyō (A.D. 419)
ARCHAIC PERIOD

Parted by the Stream

Here on one side of the stream I stand,
And gaze on my love on the other strand.
    Oh! not to be with her, what sadness!
    Oh! not to be with her, what madness!

If but a red-lacquered skiff were mine
With paddles strewn over with pearls so fine,
Then would I pass the river,
And dwell with my love forever!

                  Anonymous
                  ARCHAIC PERIOD

Rain and Snow

For ever on Mikane's crest,
    That soars so far away,
The rain it rains in ceaseless sheets,
    The snow it snows all day.

And ceaseless as the rain and snow
    That fall from heaven above,
So ceaselessly, since first we met,
    I love my darling love.

                  Anonymous
                  ARCHAIC PERIOD

Lines Composed on Beholding an Unaccompanied Damsel Crossing the Great Bridge of Kōchi

Across the bridge with scarlet lacquer glowing,
    That o'er the Katashiwa's stream is laid,
All trippingly a tender girl is going,
    In bodice blue and crimson skirt arrayed.
None to escort her: would that I were knowing
    Whether alone she sleeps on virgin bed,
Or if some spouse has won her by his wooing:—
    Tell me her house! I'll ask the pretty maid!

Anonymous
ARCHAIC PERIOD

My Love

Ah! how and by what means
    Shall I let her know of my heart?
Words are too commonplace,
    If I employed them, for the part.

Fujiwara no Sadaie, or Teika (1162–1241)
KAMAKURA PERIOD

Tell me, who is this beautiful young girl, and tell me,
   why is one so fair on this rough road?
She should be found at court, some sort of princess—O
   the grace
that gazes from her smiling eyes,
she is like the silent sky,
or like the sweet peace of the deep sea,
she is not like the people of this world.

> *from* Ikkaku Sennin,
> *a Japanese Noh play by Komparu Zempo Motoyaso*
> *(adapted by William Packard*
> *from translation of Frank Hoff)* (16TH CENTURY)
> MUROMACHI PERIOD

Peach-Blossoms

Lacking courage enough to say,
    "These peach-blossoms are just like thee!"
I simply exclaimed, and then was silent,
    "How beautiful!" admiringly.

> *Kaneko Kun-en* (20TH CENTURY)
> TOKYO PERIOD

A Verse Sent to Lady Ishikawa

While I stood waiting for my dear,
    I grew wet with the dew
Dripping down from the mountain trees;
    Yes, quite wet with the dew.

Prince Ōtsu

Lady Ishikawa's Answer

Would that I could become
    The dewdrops of the mountain tree
With which you grew so wet,
    Waiting for me.

NARA PERIOD

Love

Not the bottomless deep
    Makes any noise;
It is in the shallows
    Of a mountain brook
That idle ripples rise.

        Priest Sosei (9TH CENTURY)
        HEIAN PERIOD

The barest ledge of rock, if but a seed
Alight upon it, lets the pine-tree grow:
If, then, thy love for me be love indeed,
We'll come together, dear; it must be so!

        Anonymous
        HEIAN PERIOD

Rain on a Spring Night

How gently falls
    The fine night rain in spring!
As though the Heaven and the Earth
    Love-secrets were whispering.

Igarashi Chikara (20TH CENTURY)
TOKYO PERIOD

A man who verses writes
    With burning heart, no winter knows—
Like the camellia flower
    Which in December glows.

Yosano Hiroshi (20TH CENTURY)
TOKYO PERIOD

Love

Doubt not our love—
A phoenix bird,
Which neither cries nor flaps its wings,
Yet is alive.

Yosano Aki-ko (20TH CENTURY)
TOKYO PERIOD

Here on one side of the stream I stand,
And gaze on my love on the other strand.
   Oh! not to be with her, what sadness!
   Oh! not to be with her, what madness!

If but a red-lacquered skiff were mine
With paddles strewn over with pearls so fine,
Then would I pass the river,
And dwell with my love forever!

Falling from the ridge
of high Tsukuba,
The Minano River
At last gathers itself,
Like my love, into
A deep, still pool.

That thicket in the distance is a tower perhaps? Or a
    pleasure chamber

      Neither tower nor pleasure chamber.
         Still, a thicket is a fine place to lie in

      Better than mats. A thicket like that is the place
         for lying

      The best part of sleep on the grass is doing it two
         by two

      I brought down the one I loved in that bamboo
         grove once

from the Fourth Set of Evening Songs
in the Tauezōshi, *a medieval Japanese
cycle of songs for the annual
rice-planting festival*

If You Promise

If you promise, do it lightly.
Look at the maple leaves.
The light resist,
The heavy break away
And fall.
Is that not so?

from Songs of the Geishas

Madam Moon

The moon is disgustingly modest
Under a great cloud
When I am waiting,
And when he comes
She spitefully breaks forth.
You are jealous, Madam Moon,
But we have had a few black nights
When you were lazy.

from Songs of the Geishas

Fallen snow in the mountain
Melts in the morning sun;
Her hair
    Melts in sleep.

Japanese folk song

The man I love
And the summer blowing breeze,
I would bring in
    To my mosquito net.

Japanese folk song

Three miles brushwood mountain,
Across two miles of river, and
Coming was for whom.
>   For you.

>   *Japanese folk song*

If the wind blows
And bends the temple willows;
Won't you bend too,
>   In love's wind?

>   *Japanese folk song*

Though it rains,
I won't get wet:
I'll use your love
>   For an umbrella.

>   *Japanese folk song*

You're leaving?
I wish you wouldn't go!
I'd like to make it rain
    For ten days.

Japanese folk song

When I pick the ricefield weeds
With the man I love,
The little weeds behind us
    Are all still there.

Japanese folk song

Fog clings
To the high mountain;
My eye clings
    To him.

Japanese folk song

Snow-falling nights,
And even tea-grinding nights,
If you want me,
    Come!

                Japanese folk song

There are men you marry
And it's so boring;
There are those you don't marry,
    And love grows.

                Japanese folk song

Loveliness:
The fireflies
Light
    Our meeting's footpath.

                Japanese folk song

I want to be the Moon
And shine
On the bed
    Where he sleeps.

Japanese folk song

Everyone wants to see,
Wants to ride
A new boat
    A young girl.

Japanese folk song

Two things cannot alter,
    Since Time was, nor to-day:
The flowing of water;
    And Love's strange, sweet way.

Japanese lyric

The Cricket

Oh, cricket, chirruping
    Under my bed,
Do not tell other men
    My whispers with my beloved.

       Kagawa Kageki (1768–1843)
       YEDO PERIOD

The little fox, hidden in the garden,
Taking advantage of the darkness of the night,
   comes out.
And, sheltered by the autumn vines,
Slyly steals the grapes, already wet with dew.
Love, perhaps, is not the fox,
And thou, surely, art not the grapes.
But my heart has stolen thee away,
Secretly . . . no one knows . . .

     Shimazaki Tōson (20TH CENTURY)
     TOKYO PERIOD

Oh, how joyous, open-hearted,
Close and home-like is our love:
Sweetly secret all its ways.
Secret, too, I wish to keep it,
Yet a longing almost bursts me
To boast of it to the world.

Gonnoské Komai (20TH CENTURY)
TOKYO PERIOD

To have missed you
Even for a day
Appears to me
Like a thousand years.

If you leave me
The cold spring seems to sob;
If you come to me
Moonbeams fill my room.

Gonnoské Komai (20TH CENTURY)
TOKYO PERIOD

The Seventh Night of the Seventh Moon

Since the hour when first begun
Heaven and earth their course to run,
Parted by the Heav'nly River
Stand the Herdboy and the Weaver:
For in each year these lovers may
Meet but for one single day.
To and fro the constant swain
Wanders in the heavenly plain
Till sounds the hour when fore and aft
He's free to deck his tiny craft
In gallant trim, and ship the oar
To bear him to the opposing shore.
  Now the autumn season leads,
When through the swaying, sighing reeds
Rustles the chill breath of even,
And o'er the foaming stream of heaven,
Heedless of the silv'ry spray,
He'll row exulting on his way,
And, with his arms in hers entwin'd,
Tell all the loving tale he pin'd
To tell her through the livelong year.
  Yes! The seventh moon is here;
And I, though mortal, hail the night
That brings heaven's lovers such delight.

Ancient legend

A memory of nothingness . . .

Reminiscence

Passionate music of the Nightingale,
Not Joy you bring me, but a strange Regret,
A memory of nothingness, the pale
Face of a lover I have never met.

> *Priest Sosei* (9TH CENTURY)
> HEIAN PERIOD

That spring night I spent
Pillowed on your arm
Never really happened
Except in a dream.
Unfortunately I am
Talked about anyway.

> *Lady Suo* (11TH CENTURY)
> HEIAN PERIOD

Since that first night when, bath'd in hopeless tears,
I sank asleep, and he I love did seem
To visit me, I welcome every dream,
Sure that they come as heav'n-sent messengers.

> *Ono no Komachi* (9TH CENTURY)
> HEIAN PERIOD

An Unrequited Love

"A heroic man should not
    Cherish an unrequited love!"
Although I said so with a sigh,
    Yet I, a silly man, still love.

> *Prince Toneri* (676–735)
> NARA PERIOD

The tolling of the bell
Evokes sadness and grief;
The regret of parting lingers
With the moon at dawn.

> *from* The Confessions of Lady Nijō
> (13TH CENTURY)
> KAMAKURA PERIOD

"He is a fool," the proverb saith, "who writes
    His name in water"—and saith true.
But greater folly, through unresting nights
    To dream of one who never dreams of you.

> *Anonymous*
> HEIAN PERIOD

Forsaken

Why should I bitter be,
    Although he cold has grown?
There was a time when he to me
    And I to him were quite unknown.

Priest Saigyo (1118–1190)
KAMAKURA PERIOD

How can I tell you, dear,
How truly I am alone?
No flowers are left on earth,
Since you are gone!

Soseki (1865–1915)
TOKYO PERIOD

An Elegy on My Wife

When she was still alive
We would go out, arm in arm,
And look at the elm trees
Growing on the embankment
In front of our house.
Their branches were interlaced.
Their crowns were dense with spring leaves.
They were like our love.
Love and trust were not enough to turn back
The wheels of life and death.
She faded like a mirage over the desert.

One morning like a bird she was gone
In the white scarves of death.
Now when the child
Whom she left in her memory
Cries and begs for her,
All I can do is pick him up
And hug him clumsily.
I have nothing to give him.
In our bedroom our pillows
Still lie side by side.
As we lay once.
I sit there by myself
And let the days grow dark.
I lie awake at night, sighing till daylight.
No matter how much I mourn
I shall never see her again.
They tell me her spirit
May haunt Mount Hagai
Under the eagles' wings.
I struggle over the ridges
And climb to the summit.
I know all the time
That I shall never see her,
Not even so much as a faint quiver in the air.
All my longing, all my love
Will never make any difference.

Kakinomoto no Hitomaro (8TH CENTURY)
NARA PERIOD

An Elegy on a Dead Mistress

From now the autumn wind
    Will coldly blow in all its might;
How can I sleep alone
    All through the livelong night?

      Ōtomo no Yakamochi (8TH CENTURY)
      NARA PERIOD

An Elegy

So this was all,
    Though, free from fears,
She and I had counted on
    A thousand years.

      Ōtomo no Yakamochi (8TH CENTURY)
      NARA PERIOD

Elegy for a Lady of the Court

Her face was tinted with the shades of autumn,
Her form was pleasing as the graceful bamboo.
Her thoughts of the future were unknown to us.
We wished her a life as long as a cable,
Not short, like the rose that blooms in the morning
And dies before evening,
Or like the mist that rises in the evening
And is dispersed at morning.
Even we, who knew her only by hearsay,
We, who only caught a glimpse of her,
Are filled with profound sadness.
What, then, must be the sorrow
Of her young husband,
Who shared her bed,
Their white arms entwined as pillows?

Desolate indeed must be his thoughts when he retires,
Despairing must be his desires.
Ah, yes, she who has escaped us
Through so premature a fate,
Was indeed like the morning rose,
Or the mist of evening.

Kakinomoto no Hitomaro (8TH CENTURY)
NARA PERIOD

The Tomb of the Maiden of Unai

The Maiden of Unai in Ashinoya,
From the tender age of eight summers
Until her flowing tresses were bound up,
Was hidden from public gaze
In safe seclusion.
Even the neighbors were never
Allowed a single glimpse.
But her beauty was so much noised abroad
That people, all eager to have a peep,
Gathered around the house, forming a fence.
Among the throng were her two suitors:
A young man of Chinu and another of Unai
Were passionate rivals in her courtship.
They challenged each other,
Grasping the hilts of their sharp-bladed swords,
And shouldering full quivers and bows of white wood.
Both declared that for her dear sake
They would plunge into water or fire—
So fierce and desperate was their rivalry.
The Maiden, seeing this, said to her mother,
"Since both of them are so eager
To win me, a humble girl,
It is impossible for me in this life
To meet the one I love;
Therefore, I think I had better
Await my lover in the hereafter."
Pining for one of the youths in secret,
She desperately quit this world.
That night she appeared in a dream
To the young man of Chinu.
He then straightway followed her to Hades.

The young man of Unai, left alone,
Raised his eyes to Heaven in despair,
Threw himself on the ground, gnashing his teeth,
And shouted in fierce anger,
"I will not yield to that fellow!
No, I will not!"
With the dagger girded on him,
He killed himself, to hie after them both.
Thereupon the relatives of the unhappy three
Met in conclave, and wishing to erect
An everlasting memorial and perpetuate
The sad story to all ages,
Built three tombs, with the Maiden's
In the midst.

On hearing of this mournful occurrence of yore,
I feel as if it had happened recently,
And shed sad tears.

Takahashi no Mushimaro (8TH CENTURY)
NARA PERIOD

Sorrow

I never wished to see your face, New Year,
And yet you come as New Years came before
A woman died, whose lovely lips and dear,
Most clear, dark eyes I shall behold no more.

Mitsune
HEIAN PERIOD

The Plum-Tree

The plum-tree planted by my wife
Whene'er I look upon,
My heart is choked with sorrow,
And my tears flow down.

Ōtomo no Tabito (664–731)
NARA PERIOD

32

A youth once loved me, and his love I spurned.
But see the vengeance of the powers above
On cold indifference: now 'tis I that love,
And my fond love, alas! is not returned.

Anonymous
HEIAN PERIOD

At night I remember him
And talk to my pillow;
Pillow, say something!
        I'm burning up!

Japanese folk song

I won't wash it—
The dress he gave me;
Love's past
        Would fade.

Japanese folk song

33

"On Parting from His Wife as He Set Out from Iwami for the Capital"

It was by the sea of Iwami
Where the clinging ivy creeps across
    the rocks,
    By the waters off Cape Kara,
A land remote as the speech of far
    Cathay—
Yes, there where the seaweed grows,
Clinging to rocks fathoms beneath the
    waves,
    And where on the stony strand
The seaweed glows like polished gems.
    My young wife dwells there,
Who like seaweed bent to the current
    of love,
    The girl who slept beside me
Soft and lithesome as the gem-like
    water plants.
    Now those nights seem few
When we held each other close in sleep.
    We parted unwillingly,
Clinging to each other like ivy creepers;
    My heart ached and swelled
Against the ribs that would hold it,
    And when my yearning drew me
To pause, look back, and see her
    once again
    Waving her sleeves in farewell,
They were already taken from my sight,
    Hidden by the leaves
Falling like a curtain in their yellow whirl
    At the crest of Mount Watari,
A crest like a wave's that bears a
    ship away.

Although I longed for her—
As for the voyaging moon when it glides
    Into a rift of clouds
That swallow it up on Mount
      Yakami, where,
        They say, men retire with their wives—
I took my lonely way, watching the sun
    Coursing through the sky
Till it sank behind the mountains.

    Though I always thought
Myself a man with a warrior's heart,
    I found that my sleeves—
Wide as they were, like our bedclothes—
Were all soaked through with tears.

ENVOYS

    My gray-white horse
Has carried me at so swift a pace
    That I have left behind
The place where my beloved dwells
Beneath the cloudland of the distant sky.
    O you yellow leaves
That whirl upon the autumn slopes—
    If only for a moment
Do not whirl down in such confusion,
That I may see where my beloved dwells.

                Kakinomoto no Hitomaro (8TH CENTURY)
                NARA PERIOD

Since that first night when, bath'd in hopeless tears,
I sank asleep, and he I love did seem
To visit me, I welcome every dream,
Sure that they come as heav'n-sent messengers.

O you yellow leaves
That whirl upon the autumn slopes—
    If only for a moment
Do not whirl down in such confusion,
That I may see where my beloved dwells.

I think of you always . . .

I wish I were close
To you as the wet skirt of
A salt girl to her body.
I think of you always.

Yamabe no Akahito (8TH CENTURY)
NARA PERIOD

With each other as beloved,
If only we sleep together,
Then, though like threshed reeds,
Things go wrong, let them go wrong—
If only we sleep together.

Prince Ki-nashi-no-Karu (A.D. 453)
ARCHAIC PERIOD

The maiden of Kohada
Of the far-away country,
Whose fame rumbled afar
Like the thunder—
Now lies by my side.

I think lovingly
Of the maiden of Kohada
Of the far-away country,
Who slept by my side
Without resisting.

*Song sung by Imperial Prince Ō-sazaki
on gaining the maiden Kaminaga-hime*
(A.D. 282) ARCHAIC PERIOD

Longing for the Emperor Ōmi

While with longing I waited—
    Waited for you—
Swaying the bamboo blinds of my house,
    The autumn wind blew.

Princess Nukada (7TH CENTURY)
NARA PERIOD

A Verse Sent to Ōtomo no Yakamochi

Although the bell has tolled,
    Warning all to "go to sleep!"
My great longings after you
    My eyelids wakeful keep.

Kasa no Iratsume (9TH CENTURY)
NARA PERIOD

Overmastered by Ardent Longings

O'ermastered by my ardent thoughts,
    My home I left and hither came, astray,
Taking no heed of mountain or of stream
    Upon my way.

Hitomaro's Collection
NARA PERIOD

39

Last Night

Only last night
    I saw my darling;
Why should I long for her
    Again this morning?

Hitomaro's Collection
NARA PERIOD

A Manly Heart

Alas, that I must own
    No manly heart is mine,
Since day and night unceasingly,
    For her in love I pine.

Hitomaro's Collection
NARA PERIOD

Like the waves that ripple
Over the rough shore
Of the sea of Ago,
My longing for you
Has no time when it is still.

Anonymous
NARA PERIOD

Lines Sent to Yakamori in Exile

The strange land is an ill place
    For my dear to live in, they say;
So come home, speedily come,
    Ere for love I pine away.

                Chikami no Otome

Written While in Exile

If there were no gods whatever,
    On earth below, in heaven above,
Then might I die without once more
    Meeting my love.

              Yakamori (8TH CENTURY)
              NARA PERIOD

Song
Asking for pearls to send home to Nara

They tell me that the fisher-girls
Who steer their course o'er Susu's brine,
Dive 'neath the waves and bring up pearls:—
Oh! that five hundred pearls were mine!

Forlorn upon our marriage-bed,
My wife, my darling sweet and true,
Must lay her solitary head
Since the sad hour I bade adieu,

No more, methinks, when shines the dawn,
She combs her dark dishevelled hair:
She counts the months since I am gone,
She counts the days with many a tear.

If but a string of pearls were mine,
I'd please her with them, and I'd say,
"With flags and orange-blossoms twine
Them in a wreath on summer's day."

Ōtomo no Yakamochi (8TH CENTURY)
NARA PERIOD

To Yakamoshi

This hand, which you took
In your sublime grasp
When you promised to love me
Eternally,
I gaze on, dying of desire.

Heguri, Lady of the Court (8TH CENTURY)
NARA PERIOD

"Composed at a Time When I Was in Love, as I Saw the Burnt-over Fields Along the Road During a Trip"

Because I feel
My passion-wasted self like fields
Withered by winter,
Can I hope for better springtime
If I am burnt away like them?

Lady Ise (9TH CENTURY)
HEIAN PERIOD

As soon as the sun
          Hides behind the verdant mountains,
Then jet-black
          Night will come.
Smiling resplendently
          Like the morning sun,
With your arms
          White as rope of *taku* fibers,
          You will embrace
My breast, thrilling with youth,
          Soft as the light snow;
We shall embrace and entwine our bodies.
Your jewel-like hands
          Will twine with mine,
And, your legs outstretched,
          You will lie and sleep.
Therefore, my lord,
          Do not yearn.
Oh god
          Ya-chi-hoko!

These are
The words,
The words handed down.

*from ancient mythological accounts
of the god Ya-chi-hoko,
spoken by the Princess Nunakawa,
whom he was wooing*

What good is life?
It is really nothing more substantial
Than the drying dew—
I would exchange it without regret
For just one night with her I love!

Ki no Tomonori (10TH CENTURY)
HEIAN PERIOD

Pressed by yearning
I set out hunting for her I love,
And since the winter wind
Is cold as it blows up from the river,
The plovers cry out in the night.

Ki no Tsurayuki (884–946)
HEIAN PERIOD

It is as the seaweed
By the shore, hidden under water
When the tides are high—
The days of seeing her are few,
And the nights of longing are many.

Love song of Prince Shio-yaki
(A.D. 724–758)
NARA PERIOD

Lying down alone,
I am so confused in yearning for you
That I have forgot
The tangles of my long black hair,
Desiring the one who stroked it clear.

Izumi Shikibu (10TH CENTURY)
HEIAN PERIOD

Sagesse

The poppy of forgetfulness I sought
That seers had told me of . . .
Then spoke the wisest: "It can ne'er be bought.
It groweth only in hearts that know not love."

Priest Sosei (9TH CENTURY)
HEIAN PERIOD

On such a night as this
When no moon lights your way to me,
I wake, my passion blazing,
My breast a fire raging, exploding flame
While within me my heart chars.

Ono no Komachi (9TH CENTURY)
HEIAN PERIOD

You do not come, and I wait
On Matsuo beach,
In the calm of evening.
And like the blazing
Water, I too am burning.

Fujiwara no Sadaie, or Teika (1162–1241)
KAMAKURA PERIOD

HE: To Hatsúse's vale I'm come,
To woo thee, darling, in thy home;
But the rain rains down apace,
And the snow veils ev'ry place,
And now the pheasant 'gins to cry,
And the cock crows to the sky:
Now flees the night, the night hath fled,
Let me in to share thy bed!

SHE: To Hatsúse's vale thou'rt come,
To woo me, darling, in my home;
But my mother sleeps hard by,
And my father near doth lie;
Should I but rise, I'll wake her ear;
Should I go out, then he will hear:
The night hath fled! it may not be,
For our love's a mystery!

Ancient love song

What I like to lie beside. The body of the young
   girl. It is soft firm flesh

Say what you will, I never get tired of that
   young girl's body

Sleep with her one night and you're mixed up
   seven days after. The body of the young
   girl is beautiful.

> *from the* First Set of Evening Songs
> *in the* Tauezōshi,
> *a medieval Japanese cycle of songs*
> *for the annual rice-planting festival*

The white sleeve has picked up a scent of musk
     I slept with Lady Kuruhara. The scent
       came off
Musk, perfumes adhere. The whole sleeve smells.
Go ahead say what you will. I'm not likely to
   forget Lady Kuruhara

Never ever to forget that look, her hair still matted
   from our sleep together.

> *from the* Fourth Set of Evening Songs
> *in the* Tauezōshi

In my breast
A pained flame burns,
But no smoke rises,
    So no one knows.

Japanese folk song

More than the cicada
Who sings her burning love,
The silent firefly
    Burns

Japanese folk song

Longing in love:
When there's no other hope,
Try tying
    A rice-leaf-knot.

Japanese folk song

When your blood boils
Do what you will;
I've given this body
   To you.

> *Japanese folk song*

Just because of the milling
I touch your hand;
Without the milling, a staring fool,
   A longing fool.

> *Japanese folk song*

Love and Jealousy

Can you fancy how I love you?
Oh, mock me not, my love!
For I love you so consumingly
That my loving turns to hate
Of him who dares to love you,
And perhaps still more of him
Who presumptuously refrains.

> *Gonnoské Komai* (20TH CENTURY)
> TOKYO PERIOD

Never even to have touched
The hot blood
Of a soft body,
Doesn't it make you unhappy,
You who preach morality?

Yosano Akiko (1874–1941)
TOKYO PERIOD

tiptoeing
through the cold
suddenly
in the squeaky hallway
her mouth on mine

Ishikawa Takuboku (1885–1912)
TOKYO PERIOD

Passionate Love

I wish to feel a love
Which might be likened to
Burying a hot cheek
In a soft drift of snow

Ishikawa Takuboku (1885–1912)
TOKYO PERIOD

That which fades away . . .

That which fades away
Without revealing its altered color
Is, in the world of love,
That single flower which blossoms
In the fickle heart of man.

Ono no Komachi (9TH CENTURY)
HEIAN PERIOD

Now if it be even so,
That his love for me is done,
To some mountain peak I'll go,
For my pillow find a stone,
There to lie—and die—alone.

Empress Iha-no-hime (died A.D. 347)
ARCHAIC PERIOD

Thousands of Little Birds

About the gateway of my house,
To eat the berries of the nettle-tree,
Thousands of little birds come flocking, but
You do not come to me.

Anonymous
NARA PERIOD

In the empty mountains
The leaves of the bamboo grass
Rustle in the wind.
I think of a girl
Who is not here.

Kakinomoto no Hitomaro (8TH CENTURY)
NARA PERIOD

I have not met my beloved
For such a long time
As conspicuous as the crystal dew
Causing the foliage to change color
On the autumn mountains.

Prince Nagata (died A.D. 737)
NARA PERIOD

I should not have waited.
It would have been better
To have slept and dreamed,
Than to have watched night pass,
And this slow moon sink.

Lady Akazome no Emon (11TH CENTURY)
HEIAN PERIOD

If breezes on Inaba's peak
    Sigh through the old pine tree,
To whisper in my lonely ears
    That thou dost pine for me,—
Swiftly I'll fly to thee.

> *The Imperial Adviser Ariwara no Yukihira*
> (810–893)
> HEIAN PERIOD

. . . For a night of love
The eager girls quietly push open
    their wooden doors,
And their lovers grope, then clasp
    The hands they sought,
And sleep, beloved arms entwined

But such nights are few
And soon the lover goes with age's
    hand-staff
Carried by his side . . .

> *Yamanoue Okura (660–733) fragment from*
> *"Lament on the Instability of Human Life"*
> NARA PERIOD

Message Sent to Lady Nijō

The sorrow, the heart's hurt—
Words cannot render this.
I saw her so briefly,
The woman of my dreams.

Her Reply

Will your heart change?
I do not know.
Indifferently I watch
Chrysanthemums fade.

from The Confessions of Lady Nijō
(13TH CENTURY)
KAMAKURA PERIOD

With nothing but a memory,
How can your love persist?
Departed from this sad world
Is the dawn moon.

from The Confessions of Lady Nijō
(13TH CENTURY)
KAMAKURA PERIOD

Has it dried up?
The hidden current
Flowing in our hearts—
We never seem to meet
Despite our pledge of love.

from The Confessions of Lady Nijō
(13TH CENTURY)
KAMAKURA PERIOD

White plum tree, where can my loved
  one be?
How the scent of your blossoms brings back
  to me
The thrill of a memory you share with me—
  But the pale spring moon is cold!

Fujiwara no Ietaka (1158–1237)
KAMAKURA PERIOD

From long ago
I had heard that to meet in love
  Could only mean to part,
And yet I gave myself to you
Unconscious of the coming dawn.

Fujiwara Teika (1162–1241)
KAMAKURA PERIOD

Withered, all withered,
The grasses by the path he took to me,
  And rarer, yet rarer
Visits no longer leaving footprints
As frost grips all my house and me.

Daughter of Shunzei (13TH CENTURY)
KAMAKURA PERIOD

The Fisher Boy Urashima

'Tis Spring, and the mists come stealing
    O'er Suminóye's shore,
And I stand by the seaside musing
    On the days that are no more.

I muse on the old-world story,
    As the boats glide to and fro,
Of the fisher boy Urashima,
    Who a-fishing loved to go;

How he came not back to the village
    Though seven suns had risen and set,
But rowed on past the bounds of ocean,
    And the sea-god's daughter met;

How they pledged their faith to each other,
    And came to the Evergreen Land,
And entered the sea-god's palace
    So lovingly hand in hand,

To dwell for aye in that country,
    The ocean-maiden and he,—
The country where youth and beauty
    Abide eternally.

But the foolish boy said, "To-morrow
    I'll come back with thee to dwell;
But I have a word to my father,
    A word to my mother to tell."

The maiden answered, "A casket
    I give into thine hand;
And if that thou hopest truly
    To come back to the Evergreen Land,

HE: To Hatsúse's vale I'm come,
To woo thee, darling, in thy home;
But the rain rains down apace,
And the snow veils ev'ry place,
And now the pheasant 'gins to cry,
And the cock crows to the sky:
Now flees the night, the night hath fled,
Let me in to share thy bed!

SHE: To Hatsúse's vale thou'rt come,
To woo me, darling, in my home;
But my mother sleeps hard by,
And my father near doth lie;
Should I but rise, I'll wake her ear;
Should I go out, then he will hear:
The night hath fled! it may not be,
For our love's a mystery!

And he lifts the lid, and there rises
   A fleecy, silvery cloud,
That floats off to the Evergreen Country:—
   And the fisher boy cries aloud...

...a sudden chill comes o'er him
   That bleaches his raven hair,
And furrows with hoary wrinkles
   The form erst so young and fair....
from the legend of The Fisher Boy Urashima

"Then open it not, I charge thee!
    Open it not, I beseech!"
So the boy row'd home o'er the billows
    To Suminóye's beach.

But where is his native hamlet?
    Strange hamlets line the strand.
Where is his mother's cottage?
    Strange cots rise on either hand.

"What, in three short years since I left it,"
    He cries in his wonder sore,
"Has the home of my childhood vanished?
    Is the bamboo fence no more?

"Perchance if I open the casket
    Which the maiden gave to me,
My home and the dear old village
    Will come back as they used to be."

A fleecy, silvery cloud,
That floats off to the Evergreen Country:—
    And the fisher boy cries aloud;
And he lifts the lid, and there rises

He waves the sleeve of his tunic,
    He rolls over on the ground,
He dances with fury and horror,
    Running wildly round and round.

But a sudden chill comes o'er him
    That bleaches his raven hair,
And furrows with hoary wrinkles
    The form erst so young and fair.

His breath grows fainter and fainter,
    Till at last he sinks dead on the shore;
And I gaze on the spot where his cottage
    Once stood, but now stands no more.

Ancient Legend

When You Depart

When you have gone away,
　　No flowers more, methinks, will be—
No maple leaves in all the world—
　　Till you come back to me.

Yanagiwara Yasu-ko (1783–1866)
YEDO PERIOD

never even noticed
the misspellings
then—
an old
love letter!

Ishikawa Takuboku (1885–1912)
TOKYO PERIOD

The girl who promised
To meet me
On Mount Tsukuba—
Was it because she listened to someone else?—
Did not meet and sleep with me.

This night
When I must sleep
On Mount Tsukuba
Without a partner—
Would that it would soon dawn!

Ancient song

My lover left the Capital yesterday

    I expect him to arrive today by the road
       along the river bank through Harima

  The highway through Harima. There's a short cut

  But to go the long way round by the Harima
    road. He can't be thinking much of me

       from First Set of Evening Songs
       of the Tauezōshi,
       a medieval Japanese cycle of songs
       for the annual rice-planting festival

Looking . . . I look all around . . .
Poling my boat I've come;
Why is my love
    Not here?

Japanese folk song

Even nights when I sleep alone
I set the pillows side by side:
One is my love—
    Holding it close, I sleep.

Japanese folk song

Who gave you
The red sleeve-cord?
A man who swore his love—
    One night.

Japanese folk song

Like May rains
You came for love;
Now, water drained
 From autumn fields.

     Japanese folk song

My love
Burns like grass,
But he doesn't love me
 So much.

     Japanese folk song

"In lives to come!" you swore;
Now again you're bored;
If I could hammer nails through
 That new woman!

     Japanese folk song

"Love! Love!"
Burning, I came—and
Are you dumb,
     Saying nothing?!

Japanese folk song

No good? Fine!
You want me? Too bad!
I've got
     Other good ones.

Japanese folk song

O Dreams

O dreams, do not bring me
The face of my girl in sleep.
My waking and my pain
Would quite unman me.

from Songs of the Geishas

First Snow

This first snow
Is very white
Like first love.
My maid asks from the doorstep:
"Where shall I throw
The tea-leaves?"

from Songs of the Geishas

The maze of love

Even the nightingale
That has lost its way
In the mist of the spring hills
Not more baffled is
Than I by the maze of love.

Kakinomoto no Hitomaro (8TH CENTURY)
NARA PERIOD

Unknown Love

How full of pain is love unknown!
A "lady-lily" blooming
Amidst luxuriant grasses,
Upon the summer moor—alone!

Sakano-e no Iratsume (8TH CENTURY)
NARA PERIOD

My Heart

I said that I would not love you;
    But despite these words on my part,
I cannot but love. Like *hanezu* dye,
    How changeable is my heart!

                    Sakano-e no Iratsume (8TH CENTURY)
                    NARA PERIOD

Today and Tomorrow

Tomorrow I shall be
    Forgotten quite by thee;
Oh well, if I might die today
    While yet thou lovest me!

                    Akazome no Emon (11TH CENTURY)
                    HEIAN PERIOD

Not even in dreams
Dare I show my face to him henceforth:
Day by day my shame
Increases as the image in my mirror
Reveals new ravages of love.

Lady Ise (9TH CENTURY)
HEIAN PERIOD

Through the blackest shadow
Of the darkness of the heart I wander
In bewilderment—
You who know the world of love, decide:
Is my love reality or dream?

Ariwara Narihira (825–880)
HEIAN PERIOD

I am at one with spring:
Neither sleeping, nor yet rising from
    my bed,
    Till night turns into dawn,
And through the day my love for you
    continues
In listless looking at the ceaseless rains.

Ariwara Narihira (825–880)
HEIAN PERIOD

It cannot be borne,
One cannot shut love up in the heart—
    So let my soul-thread
Break and scatter wantonly:
Let none be shocked by what I do.

Ki no Tomonori (10TH CENTURY)
HEIAN PERIOD

Oh! Kwannon, Patron of this hill,
　　　The maid for whom I pine
Is obstinate and wayward, like
　　　The gusts around thy shrine.
　　　What of those prayers of mine?

The Minister Toshi-Yori Minamoto
KAMAKURA PERIOD

My doubt about his constancy
　　　Is difficult to bear;
Tangled this morning are my thoughts,
　　　As is my long black hair.
　　　I wonder—Does he care?

Lady Horikawa, in attendance on
the Dowager Empress Taiken
KAMAKURA PERIOD

74

As fickle as the mountain gusts
    That on the moor I've met,
'Twere best to think no more of thee,
And let thee go. But yet
I never can forget.

Daini no Sammi
KAMAKURA PERIOD

Though love, like blisters made from leaves
    Grown on Mount Ibuki,
Torments me more than I can say,
    My lady shall not see
    How she is paining me.

The Minister Sanekata Fujiwara
KAMAKURA PERIOD

A Lifeless Life

If the flame of our Love
Once ceased to burn,
Ah, how hideously cold
This world would be.

Gonnoské Komai (20TH CENTURY)
TOKYO PERIOD

A Jealous Bride

My bride at dawn a rosebud plucked
That breathed the morning air,
Then looking in her glass, she placed
That rival in her hair,
And asked me, pouting saucily,
"Which is the lovelier, say?"
But piqued, I answered jestingly,
"Of course, the flower of May!"
My lovely bride in anger cried,
And crushed the flower's charms.
"Hereafter take, instead of me,
Such rosebuds in your arms!"

Gonnoské Komai (20TH CENTURY)
TOKYO PERIOD

In the rapids where rivers meet, the boy dropped his flute

Set up the weir. Set up the weir. The
flute will come to rest in its net

Don't blow the bamboo flute of love. The sound
terrifies me

When the boy stole in to love he blew his flute

from Second Set of Evening Songs
of the Tauezōshi,
*a medieval Japanese cycle of songs
for the annual rice-planting festival*

When thread gets tangled, you can set it free again, yet . . .
People tangled together. It's not so easy
to untangle that.
Not so easy to untangle. Lovers enmeshed
A pair of wine bottles set side by side. Intimacy
Too much intimacy and a third party's interest
cools off rapidly.

from the Fourth Set of Evening Songs
in the Tauezōshi

The doctor,
The waters of Arima,
Won't repair
    Love's illness.

Japanese folk song

Though I'm scolded
"Foolishness! Nonsense!"
I can't get over
    Love's darkness.

Japanese folk song

Deep Light

I have no wish for
A frivolous or coquettish existence,
I want the deep life of love.

I have set up the double screen
Against a wind balmed with the plum trees.

Come to me and I will love you
In the tender light of the veiled moon,
I will love you, far from the plum trees.

Yet afterwards in bed
I know I shall sulk and weep;
Frogs in the garden pool
All night, all night.

from Songs of the Geishas

Who Loves

A body that loves
Is fragile and uncertain,
A floating boat.
The fires in the fishing boats at night
Burn red, my heart burns red.
Wooden stakes hold up the nets
Against the tide of Uji.

The tide is against me.

from Songs of the Geishas

Getting Out of Bed

He rises and goes. There are
Rather dark clouds.
Shall I be noisy cricket
Or firefly burning in silence,
Dumb grief or tearful parting?

And when I think we might
Never have met,
Been utter strangers.

from Songs of the Geishas

Green Willow

The breeze is so light
That when it soothes the green willow
It seems not to touch her.
Indistinct shadow.
We have set our two pillows
Very close in the bed.

Our mornings and our evenings.

And our useless little quarrels
And then our letters.
Is waiting or parting bitterer?

Let us not separate.

from Songs of the Geishas

Unstable Love

Love is unstable. I dream of a drifting
Barque. My body is limited.
My thought is infinite.
Things do not go as I would have them.
I see him in the dream of a light sleep
Or resting on one arm in place of a pillow.
Audible are the bells of Mii.

from Songs of the Geishas

Tamagava River

I bathed my snow skin
In pure Tamagava River.
Our quarrel is loosened slowly,
And he loosens my hair.
I am all uncombed.
I will not remember him,
    I will not altogether forget him,
        I will wait for Spring.

from Songs of the Geishas

Night Rain

Sad night rain, I count the straws in the mat,
He will come, he won't come.
I twist a paper frog. Does it stand?
It falls down.
A vague presentiment.
The little lamp goes down and up,
Its oil exhausted.
He was always capricious.
Ah, my soul, that is his voice.

from Songs of the Geishas

Return

I know she is light and faithless,
But she has come back half repentant
And very pale and very sad.
A butterfly needs somewhere to rest
At evening.

from Songs of the Geishas

My bride at dawn a rosebud plucked
That breathed the morning air,
Then looking in her glass, she placed
That rival in her hair,
And asked me, pouting saucily,
"Which is the lovelier, say?"
But piqued, I answered jestingly,
"Of course, the flower of May!"
My lovely bride in anger cried,
And crushed the flower's charms.
"Hereafter take, instead of me,
Such rosebuds in your arms!"

At Katushika the river water
Runs gently, and the plum blossom
Burst out laughing.
The nightingale cannot withstand so many joys
And sings, and we are reconciled.
Our warm bodies touch,
Cane branch and pine branch,
          Our boat floats in toward the bank.

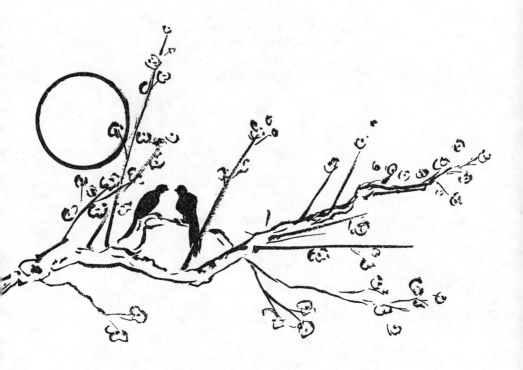

Together . . .

Until you're a hundred,
Until I'm ninety-nine,
Together
      Until white hair grows.

Japanese folk song

With you I would cross
Hell's log bridge:
Falling, swept away,
      Together in the next world.

Japanese folk song

Nightingales in the plum tree,
Deer in the maples
Me and you:
      Fish and water.

Japanese folk song

Tea mountain's tea country;
If there's tea, it's marriage country;
I'll send my girl
    Tea-picking.

Japanese folk song

Gladly I'll live in a poor mountain hut,
    Spin, sew, and till the soil in any weather,
And wash in the cold mountain stream, if but
    We dwell together.

Japanese lyric

Katushika

At Katushika the river water
Runs gently, and the plum blossom
Bursts out laughing.
The nightingale cannot withstand so many joys
And sings, and we are reconciled.
Our warm bodies touch,
Cane branch and pine branch,
    Our boat floats in toward the bank.

from Songs of the Geishas

Spring All in Flower

Spring all in flower
And the dark stain of the pine forest
On the watershed of the Sumida.
The gracious cherry trees reflected
In that deep water, which is love.
Today two Chinese ducks
Float in the thread of the current,
And I too am married.

from Songs of the Geishas

The Horse

Along the Yamashiro road
The other women's husbands travel all by horse,
But mine on foot must hold his course.
Seeing this sight I weep for him,
My heart is pained.
O husband, this bright mirror take,
Which was my mother's last bequest—
This scarf too, like the wings of dragonflies;
And with them purchase you a horse; 'tis my request.

The Reply

Suppose I buy a horse;
      You then must walk while I can ride.
Though we tread a stormy track,
      My dear, let us walk side by side.

Anonymous
NARA PERIOD

In an Emergency

O, my husband, think no anxious thoughts!
    In an emergency
Would I not plunge into fire or water
    Willingly?

Abe no Iratsume
NARA PERIOD

A Blessed Man

He is indeed a man
    Upon happiness' height,
Who can hear his wife's voice
    Till his black hair grows white.

Anonymous
NARA PERIOD

Death had no terrors, Life no joys,
        Before I met with thee;
But now I fear however long
        My life may chance to be,
        'Twill be too short for me!

Yoshitaka Fujiwara
KAMAKURA PERIOD

How desolate my former life,
        Those dismal years, ere yet
I chanced to see thee face to face;
        'Twere better to forget
Those days before we met.

The Imperial Adviser Yatsu-Tada
KAMAKURA PERIOD

Flowers

Today it seems to me that all my friends
    Have won distinction more than I in life,
However, I have flowers bought
    And love my wife.

Ishikawa Takuboku (1885–1912)
TOKYO PERIOD

Useless Vows

Though his long absence angers me,
And all my will resists his pleading,
No sooner his gay smile I see
Than—all my former vows unheeding—
His longing look my sore heart warms
And soon I'm locked within his arms.

Gonnoské Komai (20TH CENTURY)
TOKYO PERIOD

Lines Written When Leaving a Banquet

Okura will now take leave;
    For, at my home, you see,
My children may be crying, and
    Their mother waits for me.

        Yamanoue no Okura (660–733)
        NARA PERIOD

Making a mountain paddy,
Because the mountain is high,
An irrigation pipe is run
Underneath the ground, secretly—

    Secretly I have visited
        My beloved;
    Secretly I have wept
        For my spouse.

Tonight at last
    I fondle her body with ease.

        Prince Ki-nashi-no-Karu (A.D. 453)
        ARCHAIC PERIOD

The Bamboo Flute by the Shore

I

In the shade of the firs of the craggy cliff,
To-night again a bamboo flute is heard:
Is it some fisher-boy, solacing his heart
From the woes of a world bitter with salt and seaweed?

Moonlight or dark, he little cares,
Night after night he visits these fir-trees' shade.
In the music of his bamboo flute
There may be heard cadences which tell of yearning love.

A day had passed since the courtiers of the lord of the land
Held night-long revel here, wandering forth upon the beach,
While the bark of the autumn moon
Pursued its crystal course;
When the fisher's flute was for the first time heard.

II

On nights when the dew lay heavy on the reeds of the chilly shore,
And the wind of the firs came in gusts down from the crags,
He never failed to come—this fisher-boy:
His bamboo flute was heard in clear-sounding notes.

On nights when the rattling of the hail was loud,
And the ripples on the beach were changed to ice,
He never failed to come—this fisher-boy:
His bamboo flute was heard in subdued tones.

On nights when evening fell, wild with mountain blasts,
And the sand was whirled up into the air,
He never failed to come—this fisher-boy:
His bamboo flute was heard in confused notes.

On nights of rain, when darkness came down with a sound of
   moaning waves,
And the rocks were steeped in moisture,
He never failed to come—this fisher-boy:
His bamboo flute was heard, languid and faint.

III

To-night the autumn moon has changed,
So long his yearning love has endured.
Still his bamboo flute is heard,
Its tune and measure ever more entrancing.

With the storm from the cliff it was troubled,
With the echoes from the fir-trees it became clear,
With the surges from the deep it was frenzied,
With the waves on the rocks it became choked.

Even the clouds over Onoye paused to listen
To its notes, now calling clearly, and now with strangled utterance,
What wonder then that some one descends from the bower above,
And comes forth absorbed in reverie!

For a while the flute ceased its importunities;
But hark! louder than before
The music of the bamboo bursts forth, making the sky resound,
And in accord with it, how sweet!
Are heard the notes of a golden lute.

Sometime the wide-spreading clouds descending from Onoye
Bore away with them the musicians of the fragrant rocks below,
Up to that region where the barque of the moon,
With altered helm, steered straight to meet them.

Shiwoi Ukō
TOKYO PERIOD

Sun goes down. Against it two snipe fly westward

        There's a lake in the west too, they say

Along the pond deep in the hills into which the
    snipe plummeted down

Are birds making love? Their cries are pitched so high

Two, paired. Close-set. That's what it is to be
    together

> *from* Fourth Set of Evening Songs
> *in the* Tauezōshi,
> *a medieval Japanese cycle of songs
> for the annual rice-planting festival*

The path we have climbed has been steep and hard,
Though the two of us walked together;
How can you go on now alone, dear heart,
Through the chill of the autumn weather?

> *Princess Daihaku* (7TH CENTURY)
> ARCHAIC PERIOD

Index of First Lines